SANKOFA
BLACK HERITAGE COLLECTION

HOPES AND DREAMS

NICOLE RICKETTS

SERIES EDITOR • TOM HENDERSON

ADVISORY BOARD

Nicole Aloise
Vice-Principal at Weston Collegiate Institute
Toronto District School Board, Ontario

Tom Henderson
Curriculum Consultant
African Canadian Services Division
Nova Scotia Department of Education
and Early Childhood Development

Marsha Forbes
Anti-Racism and Equity Chair
Peel Elementary Teachers' Local, Ontario

Sharon Moss
Principal of Leadership Development
York Region District School Board, Ontario

www.rubiconpublishing.com

Copyright © 2015 Rubicon Publishing Inc. Published by Rubicon Publishing Inc. All rights reserved. No part of this publication may be reproduced, stored in a database or retrieval system, distributed, or transmitted in any form or by any means, electronic, mechanical, photocopying, recording, or otherwise, without the prior written permission of Rubicon Publishing Inc.

Associate Publisher: Amy Land
Project Editor: Jessica Rose
Creative Director: Jennifer Drew
Lead Designer: Sherwin Flores
Graphic Designers: Roy Casim, Jennifer Harvey, Brandon Koepke, Megan Little, Jason Mitchell

Every reasonable effort has been made to trace the owners of copyrighted material and to make due acknowledgement. Any errors or omissions drawn to our attention will be gladly rectified in future editions.

15 16 17 18 19   5 4 3 2 1

ISBN: 978-1-77058-832-5

Printed in China

CONTENTS

4 **Introduction: Hopes and Dreams**

6 **Dreaming Big**
These quotations may help to inspire you to reach for your hopes and dreams.

8 **The Honourable Jean Augustine: Leading the Way**
This Q&A will tell you everything you need to know about Jean Augustine, the first African Canadian woman to be elected to the Canadian Parliament.

11 **Career Planning Checklist**
Choosing a career isn't always easy. This checklist will help you to plan for the future.

12 **Beyond the Rhythm**
Whether you dream of becoming a poet or a scientist, this poem by Joan Butterfield will remind you anything is possible.

14 **Dwight Drummond: News Reporter**
Dwight Drummond didn't know what to expect when he moved to Canada as a child. Read this profile to see how he achieved his dreams.

18 **A Canadian I Admire**
In this opinion piece, you'll read about why it is important to educate young girls around the world.

20 **Michaëlle Jean Speaks on International Women's Day**
Former Governor General Michaëlle Jean believes everybody has the potential to change the world. Find out what else she believes in this speech.

24 **How Stories Came to Be**
Find out what the world was like before dreams and stories in this traditional Zulu folk tale.

28 **I Hope I Can**
What happens when Tallah doesn't get the support of her best friend? Find out in this reader's theatre script.

30 **Dreaming of Equality**
Read this report to find out how the No. 2 Construction Battalion was formed.

34 **Becky and the Wheels-and-Brake Boys**
Becky dreams of owning and riding a bike just like the Wheels-and-Brake Boys. As you'll read in this short story, she faces many obstacles.

42 **Racing to the Finish**
Braedon Dolfo didn't let the fact he is partially blind stand in the way of achieving his dream. Read about his journey in this profile.

46 **Winners Never Quit**
As you'll read in this personal account, it's important to never give up on your dreams.

48 **Acknowledgements**

HOPES AND DREAMS

It's important to dream big, whether you hope to win an Olympic gold medal or become the first teenager to fly in space. But trying to achieve your biggest dreams can sometimes be scary.

Take the advice of Ellen Johnson Sirleaf, the first female head of state in Africa. She says, "The size of your dreams must always exceed your current capacity to achieve them. If your dreams do not scare you, they are not big enough." But achieving your biggest dreams isn't always easy. There are often obstacles to overcome.

INFORMATIONAL TEXT | QUOTATIONS

DREAMING BIG

THINK ABOUT IT
Think about a quotation you have heard that you still remember. What do you think makes a quotation memorable?

EVERYONE HAS HOPES and dreams for his or her life. The following inspiring quotations by people of African descent are all about dreaming big.

"I feel I was groomed for great things, whether it was great success or great loss. I have a capacity for **extremes.**"

— Measha Brueggergosman (b. 1977), Canadian classical and opera singer

"We must realize that **our future** lies chiefly in our own hands."

— Paul Robeson (1898–1976), American actor, musician, and civil rights activist

"Hope … is the belief that our **destiny** will not be written for us, but by us, by the men and women who are not content to settle for the world as it is, who have the **courage** to remake the world as it should be."

— Barack Obama (b. 1961), 44th president of the United States

> First you **dream** and then you lace up your boots.
>
> — Portia White (1911–1968), Canadian classical singer

> Follow your **passion,** be prepared to work hard and sacrifice, and, above all, don't let anyone limit your dreams.
>
> — Donovan Bailey (b. 1967), Canadian Olympic gold medallist in track and field

> Bringing the gifts that my ancestors gave, I am the dream and the hope of the slave. **I rise. I rise. I rise.**
>
> — Maya Angelou (1928–2014), American poet

> When I look down at this golden statue, may it remind me and every little child that no matter where you're from, your **dreams** are valid.
>
> — Lupita Nyong'o (b. 1983), Academy Award–winning Kenyan actor

> I'll go **anywhere** as long as it's **forward.**
>
> — Malcolm Gladwell (b. 1963), Canadian journalist and author, based in New York

CONNECT IT

Use the Web to research one of the people quoted in this selection. Write a profile that includes information about the person's hopes and dreams and what he or she has accomplished. Include information about why this person's quotation is memorable.

INFORMATIONAL TEXT | Q&A

The Honourable Jean Augustine:
Leading the Way

THINK ABOUT IT

What qualities do you think someone must have in order to be an influential politician? Write a list of adjectives.

JEAN AUGUSTINE HAS had a successful career as a Canadian educator, community organizer, and politician. From her early years in Grenada, where she was born, to her illustrious career in politics, she has inspired many people. In 1993, she became the first Black woman to be elected to Canada's Parliament. Read about this accomplishment and more in the following Q&A.

illustrious: *memorable; respected*

What was Jean Augustine's childhood like?

Jean Augustine was born in Grenada, an island nation located in the Caribbean Sea, in 1937. When she was very young, Augustine's father died. An older woman in the village, whom Augustine called Granny, adopted her. Granny encouraged Augustine to get an education, which made Augustine one of the only educated people in her village.

What was life like for Augustine when she first arrived in Canada?

Augustine came to Canada in 1960 when she was 22. Although she was trained and licensed as a teacher in Grenada, she could not teach in Canada because her credentials were not recognized. Instead, she worked as a nanny. While working as a nanny, she also went to school to get an Ontario Teaching Certificate. She graduated in 1963. Later, she earned a Bachelor of Arts and a Master of Education from the University of Toronto.

What happened next?

Augustine became a teacher and later a principal. She also volunteered for a number of community organizations. While volunteering, she saw many people living in poverty and facing other hardships. She thought the best way to create change was to enter politics. In 1993, she became the first Black woman to be elected a Member of Parliament. "I didn't run as a Black politician," she said of the achievement. "I ran as a competent woman who is Canadian." She was a Member of Parliament until 2006.

What did Augustine accomplish while a Member of Parliament?

As a politician, Augustine achieved many things. Some achievements were connected to her passion for social justice and equality. She acted as Parliamentary Secretary to Prime Minister Jean Chrétien, Chair of the National Liberal Women's Caucus, and Secretary of State for Multiculturalism and the Status of Women. In 1995, she introduced a motion to declare February Black History Month in Canada. It was passed unanimously by Parliament in 1995.

Where is she now?

Augustine retired in March 2015 from her job as the first Fairness Commissioner for Ontario. She had had this job since March 2007. One role of the Fairness Commission is to help people who come to Ontario with professional qualifications from other countries to get a licence to work in Canada. Augustine worked with a team to help people such as doctors and teachers overcome obstacles to fulfilling their professional dreams.

Caucus: *group of people within a political party that share concerns*
motion: *legal action or process*
unanimously: *without opposition*

Jean Augustine

Find out more information about the Fairness Commission. How does it support new Canadians? Why is its role important?

What advice does Augustine have for young people?

In 2011, Augustine accepted an honorary doctorate from York University. This is part of the speech she made to young teacher graduates:

Enjoy the moment.

I know it feels like you've crossed the finish line, but actually it's more a threshold. Graduation marks a starting point, rather than the end of your academic studies.

Sorry to be the one to bring you the news.

I can speak from an experience of 35 years in educational settings. I can tell you that education is not something you do, it is something you live.

Learning never stops, should never stop, and is not a destination but rather a journey. Think of it as one big conversation.

The reality is you are now the next generation of educators with the power to create, to shape, and respond to the future.

You can help Ontario and you can help Canada manage and coordinate innovation.

But what is special about you, graduating class, is your sense of connectedness — no fear that you're taking the journey alone.

You are the millennials.

You are the wired generation, born at the dawn of the WWW, and technology has never been foreign to you. In fact, technology is part of your DNA. … It's what you know.

But for the rest of us, my age and older, you are a generation that has us guessing.

And so as I look out at you and I see the bright, smiling faces, taking delight in your accomplishments, I can only imagine what it means to you to hear that this isn't about finishing your studies as much as it is about starting to learn and to find your place in the world. … Convocation is a launch pad, not an arrivals area.

> Why might Augustine choose to use the word "millennials" instead of students or young people?

> What might Augustine mean when she says, "Convocation is a launch pad, not an arrivals area"? Write it in your own words.

CONNECT IT

Choose one sentence from Augustine's speech that you find inspirational. Write a journal entry about why you find that excerpt inspirational.

INFORMATIONAL TEXT | CHECKLIST

Career Planning Checklist ☑

THINK ABOUT IT

What's your dream job? What are some things you could start doing now to prepare for having this job in the future?

IT CAN TAKE a lot of work to achieve your career goals. Read this checklist to learn how you can start preparing for the future today.

☑ Work hard at school.

Developing good study habits and doing your homework can help you in the future. In most jobs, it's important to be organized, attentive, and accurate. Studying and doing your homework help to teach you these skills.

☑ Consider your skills and interests.

Think about the things you're really good at doing and that interest you. Your skills and interests can help you narrow down jobs you might be suited for in the future.

☑ Talk to people in the field.

Networking with people who already do the job you dream of doing is a great way to decide if you have what it takes. Ask them the following questions:

- Why did you decide to pursue this job?
- What kind of education did you need to attain?
- What do you like most about your job?
- What, if anything, do you dislike about your job?

☑ Ask for advice.

Talk to a guidance counsellor, teacher, mentor, tutor, or family member about what you want to do when you're older. These people can give you advice about how to pursue your career hopes and dreams.

☑ Get involved in extracurricular activities.

It's never too early to start planning! Getting involved in extracurricular activities shows that you have multiple interests and that you have skills such as leadership and teamwork.

CONNECT IT

Choose one job you might be interested in doing. Do some research and make a list of three skills that might be needed to do this job. What can you do to develop each of these skills?

POETRY

Beyond the Rhythm

BY JOAN BUTTERFIELD

THINK ABOUT IT

What could the phrase "beyond the rhythm" mean?

THE POEM AND IMAGES in this selection were used as part of an exhibition called *Beyond the Rhythm*. The exhibition was curated by Joan Butterfield.

It's the rhythm of our journey that has kept us alive,
it's our strength as a people that helped us survive.

It's more than the rhythm that set us free,
we are more than what you imagine us to be.

We are people proud of who we are,
and all that we have accomplished thus far.

We do more than play ball, bop, and jive,
we have achieved much more in our lives.

We are artists, writers, and teachers, too,
read about us in the pages of *Who's Who*.

Doctors, scientists, and inventors — that's what we are,
in spite of the obstacles we have come so far.

Business owners and corporate CEOs,
actors and directors of Broadway shows.

curated: *organized by*
CEOs: *Chief Executive Officers*

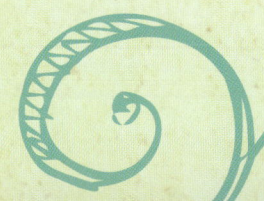

ABOUT THE POET

Joan Butterfield is a visual artist, curator, and author. She was born in Bermuda, but now lives in Brampton, Ontario. She is the creator, producer, and curator of *Beyond the Rhythm*, an art exhibit that happens each year alongside the Toronto Caribbean Carnival.

Houses in the country, condos downtown,
mega yachts floating leisurely in the sound.

We are proud mothers, fathers, and children who,
have hopes and dreams for our families, too.

We have soul food Sundays, with homemade pies,
backyard picnics under sunny skies.

Moonlight cruises, walks at sunrise,
friendly gatherings for traditional fish fries.

Our heritage is rich with stories yet untold,
our lives continue to unfold.

We are people of courage, faith, hope, and will,
with many more dreams yet to be fulfilled.

Discover — who dwells — Beyond the Rhythm.

sound: *narrow stretch or body of water*
will: *determination*

CONNECT IT

In a small group, talk about why the author of this book might have chosen to include this poem. Talk about how this poem challenges stereotypes. How can stereotypes be challenged and dispelled?

These paintings by Izzy Ohiro were part of the Beyond the Rhythm *exhibition that featured Joan Butterfield's poem.*

INFORMATIONAL TEXT | PROFILE

DWIGHT DRUMMOND:
NEWS REPORTER

GLORIA ELAYADATHUSSERIL
CANADIAN IMMIGRANT
19 MAY 2011

THINK ABOUT IT

What might make someone's immigration experience easier or more difficult? Share your thoughts with a classmate.

DWIGHT DRUMMOND WAS born in Montego Bay, Jamaica. He moved to Canada in 1976. Today, he is one of the country's most respected news reporters and anchors. Before becoming a reporter, Drummond worked at a lot of different jobs. He was a security guard, a teleprompter operator, and a cameraperson.

In this profile, Drummond doesn't talk only about his own dreams. He also talks about the dreams of his mother. Read about the sacrifices she made in order for her family to live the "Canadian dream."

What might the author mean by the "Canadian dream"? Compare this to what you know about the idea of an "American dream."

Dwight Drummond co-hosting a CBC news broadcast

Young Dwight Drummond was completely confused when he landed at Toronto's international airport. The nine-year-old expected airplanes in Canada to look like spaceships and people to have pointed ears just like Dr. Spock of the popular science fiction television series *Star Trek*.

"My mom sent me a 'View-Master' and slides of *Star Trek*," he begins to explain about the gift he received from his mom, who had moved to Canada. "I thought I was looking at slides of Canada!"

He was oblivious to most things urban, including television. … "We didn't have television [in Jamaica], and I don't think we even had electricity." But he loved his little universe: "We had a pineapple hedge around the house, a mango tree. [If you were] hungry, you climbed up the tree. … It was an idyllic kind of setting for me."

But he knew he would have to move out of his sanctuary one day. "When my mom came and visited, I knew that at some point I was going to end up in Canada."

The whole immigration experience was a bit tough on Drummond. … "Getting to Canada was difficult for me in the sense that I not only had to adjust to a new country, but a family that had been fractured and splintered — even on the island because my mom had left her four children with different people."

However, he says with gratitude, "My mom had dreams and aspirations not so much for herself, but really for her children. She really felt that Canada would offer us the opportunities that Jamaica didn't.

"And my mom really led by example. She started out in the sweatshop [on Spadina Avenue in Toronto], working her fingers to the bone. She went back to school here and upgraded her education and ended up as a nurse. Now she is living her Canadian dream," he says with pride.

> Why do you think Drummond's mother first moved to Canada by herself without him?

> What three words would you use to describe Drummond's mother?

View-Master: *toy used to view slides*
idyllic: *very happy and peaceful*
sanctuary: *protected place*
aspirations: *hopes to achieve something*
sweatshop: *place of employment where workers are often paid very little and work under poor or dangerous conditions*

15

[Drummond's dreams] didn't come true without going through hardships along the way. Drummond grew up in the Jane Street and Finch Avenue area [a Toronto neighbourhood], in a public housing community. "It wasn't always easy, there were trials and tribulations." …

Drummond ran into **racial profiling** from the police and at school. "I was one of those people who tackled it head-on. If I felt a teacher was saying an inappropriate thing, I wrote about it in my school newspaper."

> Why is the the ability to tackle issues "head-on" a good quality for a journalist?

"You're going to run into issues, especially when you are trying to adjust into a new society. The trick is not to let those issues make you bitter."

That also fired up his passion for journalism. He wanted to study at the Radio and Television Arts school at Ryerson University. "I was an Ontario Scholar, so I really had good marks, but it was so competitive to get admission," he remembers.

Drummond got in with a winning letter in which he wrote: "You want diversity? Then give me a chance! … If you are reporting about my neighbourhood, why not have somebody from the neighbourhood report on it?"

Drummond, who recently became a co-host of the *CBC News Toronto* supper-hour newscasts, has worked as both an anchor and reporter for more than 20 years. Prior to joining CBC, he worked as a crime specialist on City TV's *CityNews*.

"You're going to run into issues, especially when you are trying to adjust into a new society. The trick is not to let those issues make you bitter," he says. "No matter what stumbling blocks you run into, in the end, you will think … I'm glad I chose Canada."

racial profiling: *targeting certain individuals based on the colour of their skin*

CBC news team Anne-Marie Mediwake and Dwight Drummond

LIGHTS, CAMERA, ACTION!

Camera operator

Being a news reporter means that Dwight Drummond needs to be comfortable in front of the cameras. But don't worry! You can still dream about working in a newsroom even if you're camera-shy. These are just a few of the many jobs available behind the scenes in a newsroom.

Assignment Editor
Assignment editors assign news stories to reporters. Assignment editors assign stories based on research and press releases they have received.

Reporter
Reporters do research, interview sources, and film their news stories, which later appear on the news.

Camera Operator
Some camera operators accompany reporters to film their stories. Others work in the newsroom where they film the newscast. Some camera operators do both. They're also responsible for addressing any technical glitches that arise.

Newswriter
Newswriters write the scripts that a newscaster must follow. Newswriters compose introductions to introduce news stories. Sometimes, they also come up with the banter that takes place between newscasters.

Teleprompter Operator
You might think that newscasters have a lot of lines to remember, but chances are, they're following along to the script on a teleprompter. A teleprompter operator is the person who runs a teleprompter.

Producer
Producers make sure that everything during a newscast goes smoothly. It's their job to communicate with newscasters, production staff, and the control room. Producers do many other jobs, too, like deciding on the order of news stories.

teleprompter: *device used to project a script out of sight of an audience*

CONNECT IT
Interview someone who has come to Canada from another country. You could choose a friend, teacher, or family member. Make a list of questions you would like to ask during your interview. Remember to include questions about successes and challenges he or she has faced.

INFORMATIONAL TEXT | OPINION PIECE

A Canadian I Admire

SAMUEL GETACHEW
HUFFINGTON POST
10 NOVEMBER 2013

THINK ABOUT IT

There is an African proverb that says, "If you educate a man, you educate an individual, but if you educate a woman, you educate a family." How do you interpret this proverb?

CANADIAN ACTIVIST HANNAH GODEFA is helping girls in Ethiopia receive an education. By doing so, she's giving them the tools to achieve their hopes and dreams. Read this opinion piece to learn about the importance of educating girls around the world.

The United Nations General Assembly in New York adopted 11 October as the International Day of the Girl Child [in 2011].

The aim is that the day will mark the milestones and challenges of being a young girl. This year's theme is Innovating for Girls' Education. For me, no one represents what the day intends to celebrate more than a young Canadian friend who is making a profound impact in the country of my birth. Hannah Godefa, only 15, exemplifies the best of what it means to be an international Canadian citizen.

What an impact she is having in the world.

Eight years ago, while in Axum, Ethiopia, the then seven-year-old Maple, Ontario, resident discovered her activist spirit as she saw first-hand the poverty and shortcomings of the country of her birth. She understood that the best way to help others escape poverty is by empowering young people to get an education. She therefore decided to start an organization, which she named Pencil Mountain Project, in the hope of raising and distributing 20 000 pencils in Ethiopia.

Since then, the group has raised more than 600 000 pencils, school supplies, accessories for [children who have a disability], and thousands of books for Ethiopian universities by working with the Ethiopian Ministry of Education. Her efforts soon became a movement where, in her activism, she met many leaders involved in world affairs, including her public hero Craig Kielburger.

Students in Debre Markos, Ethiopia

Upon learning of her efforts and meeting her in person, it was Kielburger who seemed touched by her efforts.

In an article co-written with his brother, Marc Kielburger, he described the grade 9 student from Markham's St. Elizabeth Catholic High School as someone who is "warm, polite, and humble, but also dedicated, hard-working, and passionate about helping others. She loves Canada while maintaining a personal connection to the rich cultural heritage of her roots."

Late last year, she even impressed her local Member of Parliament, Julian Fantino, and she was invited to meet with Prime Minister Stephen Harper. For Fantino, Hannah was an impressive young leader who "exemplifies the meaning of community spirit and dedication. She continues to accomplish so much in support of those in need halfway across the world."

Even UNICEF also took notice of her activism and selected the teenage dynamo as its Goodwill Ambassador for Ethiopia. Upon her selection, she reflected how "it has always been my dream to help children who do not have the opportunities to reach their highest potential. The most important message I want to give to Ethiopian children is the value of education. Children are imaginative, intelligent, and valuable, and they truly can change the world if given the opportunities to learn," she added.

Today, I remember the wise words of the late Marion Dewar in celebration on this important day. "To end global poverty and injustice, we need to recognize and nurture women's leadership," Ottawa's greatest mayor [Dewar] once said. Hannah Godefa seems to understand that — not just in theory but in practice.

It is no wonder the Government of Canada awarded her the Queen's Diamond Jubilee Medal for all her efforts earlier this year. She was indeed a worthy candidate.

I am her biggest fan.

Hannah Godefa and UNICEF Executive Director Anthony Lake as Katy Perry is appointed a UNICEF Goodwill Ambassador in December 2013.

CONNECT IT

Find an organization in your own community that is trying to create change. Present your findings about the organization to the class. As a class, consider voting for one organization to support through fundraising.

A school in Ethiopia

INFORMATIONAL TEXT | SPEECH

MICHAËLLE JEAN
SPEAKS ON
INTERNATIONAL WOMEN'S DAY

THINK ABOUT IT

What do you know about International Women's Day? Why do you think it is important?

READ THE FOLLOWING speech by the Right Honourable Michaëlle Jean, 27th Governor General of Canada (2005–2010), to learn about her hopes and dreams. The speech was delivered in Vancouver on International Women's Day in 2006 to celebrate the 30th anniversary of MOSAIC. MOSAIC is a *non-profit organization* that helps immigrants and refugees settle and integrate into Canadian society.

non-profit organization: business that works to benefit the general public without the motive of making a profit

I am delighted to be here with you to celebrate MOSAIC's 30th anniversary on my first official visit to British Columbia.

It is in the spirit of friendship that I speak to you today, because I have faced the same challenges you have faced: adapting to a different culture, finding decent housing and employment. I, too, know what it means to be uprooted. I know the courage it takes to rebuild a life, far from friends and loved ones, from everything familiar. I remember the last day I spent on my native island, Haiti, which had become a prison for my family. I remember our arrival in Montreal on a cold winter's night. I remember our readiness to start over, safe at last from massacre, torture, injustice. I remember our desire, more powerful than anything else, to start living again, to dream once more.

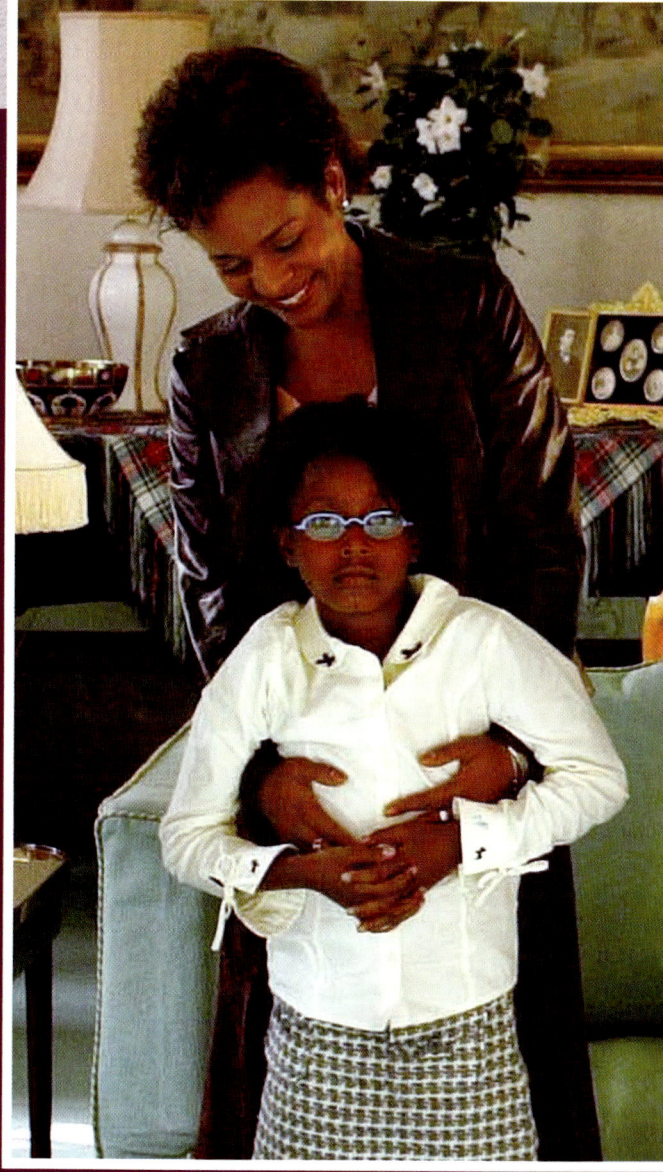

Michaëlle Jean and her daughter, Marie-Éden, 6 September 2005

> **"I would like to salute the courage of so many immigrant women who sometimes raise their families alone."**

My mother, sister, and I lived for years in a tiny basement apartment in Montreal that had just one and a half rooms. Despite the uncertainty that comes with working odd jobs, my mother held her head high, her pride and dignity never wavering. And so today, as we celebrate International Women's Day, I would like to salute the courage of so many immigrant women who sometimes raise their families alone. From our first apartment to the first house my mother bought by putting together her savings, we slowly began to put down roots. I became attached to this country, the place where I belong, the land I love.

21

> The following three questions are rhetorical questions. Rhetorical questions are questions that are not intended to be answered because the answer is obvious. Why might Jean have chosen to include rhetorical questions in her speech?

> Why do you think Jean chooses to focus on young people here?

Is that not the same story of so many immigrants and refugees in Canada? In Montreal, Toronto, or Vancouver, the longing for a better future is the same. As are the difficulties. We should not underestimate how daunting the obstacles are that immigrants must overcome. Even their children born in this country may have difficulty fully integrating into society. What about the young people torn between the weight of traditions to which their parents cling and the search for new identities? What about the youth from various backgrounds for whom the future seems almost closed off and the opportunities seem so limited that delinquency is quick to entangle them in its nets? What about those who turn to the streets, turning their backs on school?

To the young people here today, I extend my warmest greetings and cannot begin to tell you how very important it is for you to make your voices heard. I want you to share your realities with me, however troubling they may be. I want you to share your ideas with me, however provocative they may be. I want you to share your dreams for the future with me, however idealistic they may be! Because I firmly believe that the distress and despair felt by too many in our society and, unfortunately, by too many young people are the result of dialogues that never took place and never-launched debates about ideas. I believe the future starts today, and it begins with you.

daunting: *intimidating; difficult to deal with*
delinquency: *minor crime*
provocative: *challenging*
idealistic: *optimistic; unrealistic*

Students surround Michaëlle Jean during the Michaëlle Jean Public School opening ceremony, 2008.

22

Every word counts, every action matters. The volunteers and staff at MOSAIC are living proof of this. The members of MOSAIC's founding agencies shared a common dream: to help immigrants in the Greater Vancouver Area integrate into their host society by providing a complete range of services, from language courses to counselling to job-search training. Thirty years later, hundreds of employees and volunteers are keeping that dream alive with *conviction*, passion, and dedication.

> **"I encourage each person who has come here in the hope of exploring new possibilities or of starting over to take every opportunity to enliven our society with their unique contribution."**

Think of the number of people you have helped, guided, comforted. Think of the women and men who, because of you, were able to better their circumstances and thrive. Think of all of the families you have counselled, all of the young people you have given new hope. You *embody* the motto I have chosen as Governor General: "Breaking down *solitudes*." This means giving each and every one of us the capacity to utilize our potential in every aspect and to get involved, through our words and actions, in our community. This is what you are doing, day after day.

I encourage each person who has come here in the hope of exploring new possibilities or of starting over to take every opportunity to enliven our society with their unique contribution. Democracy starts from the will to take action where we live and where we choose to put down roots. In other words, in this generous country, where we have the privilege of dreaming big dreams, for the good of our loved ones and the entire community. I believe that this is what true integration really is. Integration is a *reciprocal* adventure: it is about receiving and giving. It is about rights and responsibilities.

Thank you very much for inviting me here today. Thirty years — quite an achievement! I am eager now to hear your story.

---

conviction: *firmly held belief*
embody: *symbolize*
solitudes: *states of being alone*
reciprocal: *shared; joint*

> What are some ways you have been, or can be, involved in your community?

CONNECT IT

Use the Web to learn how the Michaëlle Jean Foundation is helping young adults make their dreams come true. Share your findings in a small group.

FICTION | FOLK TALE

How Stories Came to Be

THINK ABOUT IT

Think about the stories you enjoyed as a young child. What did you like about them? In a small group, talk about what makes a story memorable.

READ ABOUT THE world before stories and dreams in this traditional Zulu folk tale.

Long ago, perhaps thousands of years ago, there lived a very wise man and his wife, who was also very wise. They lived in a small village and were loved by all the other villagers. The very wise man and his very wise wife lived happily together with their many children.

By day, the man and woman spent their time working hard on the land. The land provided for all of their needs. The long grasses were woven into baskets. Animals were hunted for food and hides. The earth was tilled for crops to be traded.

After a day of working hard, the family would gather by the fire to sit and eat before going to sleep. It would have been a good time to share stories, but this was a time before stories and dreams. The very wise woman had heard the word "stories," but she did not have any stories to tell.

The very wise woman turned to her husband for help.

"Dear husband," she said. "I want to tell the children a story, but I have none to tell. Please tell me a story." The very wise man thought and thought and thought, but he did not know a story either.

tilled: *prepared; cultivated*

The situation caused the wise couple much distress, so they went in search of someone who could give them stories to share with their children. They asked their neighbours, but their neighbours did not know any stories. They asked the other wise people in their village, but the wise people had no stories to share with them. They even asked the wind, but the wind did not have any stories, dreams, or even magic tales to share.

The wise couple's greatest dream was to find stories to share with their children.

"Whatever shall we do?" cried the wise woman.

"You must go in search of stories," said the very wise man. "Bring back every one you find." He promised to take very good care of the children and the land until she returned.

The very wise woman agreed and set off in search of stories to bring back for her people.

As she began her journey, the very wise woman thought of a plan. "I will ask every creature I meet," she said to herself. "I will keep the stories they share and bring them back to my people."

First, she met a hare. "Hello, Hare," she said. "I am a very wise woman from a village nearby, and I am in search of stories for my people. Do you know of any stories that I might have?"

"Stories during the day, indeed! How silly!"

Hare regarded her for a moment.

"Do I know any stories? I, Hare? he said, annoyed. "Of course, I know stories! I know hundreds … no, thousands … no, MILLIONS of stories!" he exclaimed.

"Please tell me some so that my people may be happy," the wise woman pleaded.

"Stories now?" said Hare. "In the middle of the day? Can you not see that I am very busy? Stories during the day, indeed! How silly!" exclaimed Hare as he hopped away.

The very wise woman sighed as she watched Hare hop away. "He probably didn't have stories anyway," she said aloud to herself and continued on her journey.

Soon, she met a mother baboon and her infants.

"Oh, Mother Baboon," called the very wise woman, "I am hoping to find stories to take back to my people. Surely, you have stories you tell your young ones. Please share them with me."

Mother Baboon stopped to look at the very wise woman. "Stories now?" yelled Mother Baboon. "Do I look like I have time to be telling anybody stories? Can't you see that I am very busy? For such a wise woman, you ask silly questions!" Mother Baboon scurried away with all her infants in tow. The very wise woman sighed.

"For such a wise woman, you ask silly questions!"

"Mother Baboon really is busy," she said aloud to herself and continued on her journey. She met an owl, an elephant, and an eagle along the way, but none of them had stories to share. Just as she was about to give up in despair, the very wise woman met a large sea turtle, and her luck seemed to change. The large sea turtle listened to her plight, and then he carried her away to the land of the Spirit People, way at the bottom of the sea.

Awe and fear overcame the very wise woman when she first saw the Spirit People. As she bowed before them, the very wise woman noticed how regal they appeared.

"Woman from the Dry Land," the Spirit People said in unison. "What can we do for you?"

"I am on a journey in search of stories to bring back to my people," the very wise woman said quietly. "Do you have any stories?"

plight: *difficulty; problem*
regal: *fit for a king or queen*

"Yes," they stated. "We have many, many stories, but what will you give us in exchange?" they inquired.

The very wise woman thought about this request for a long, long time, but she could not think of anything to exchange with the Spirit People.

Finally, she replied, "I do not know what I can exchange with you. What would you like?"

"We would like something that is near and dear to your heart. We'd like something that you treasure."

"The most near and dear things to me are my family and my home," she said after a long pause. "They are my treasure, but they are far away, so I carry a carving with me. It is of the members of my family, my home, and my village. My very wise husband made it himself," she said with pride.

The very wise woman revealed the carving to the Spirit People. The Spirit People looked at the carving with awe and wonderment. They admired her husband's fine work and gave the wise woman a special shell necklace to show their appreciation.

"Whenever you want a story," they said, "put this shell to your ear, and you will hear one." The very wise woman thanked them for their kind-heartedness and journeyed back to her own village. Her family and all the people in her village had missed the very wise woman, and they warmly welcomed her home. Her children especially had missed her. As she settled down by the huge fire, they cried, "Mama! Please tell us a story! Tell us a story, please!"

So, the very wise woman sat down. She put the shell to her ear, and began …

"Once long, long ago, there was a very wise woman who had the most marvellous dream …"

And that is how stories came to be.

CONNECT IT

This traditional tale of the Zulu people of South Africa is just one of many that have been passed down through generations. Use the Web and other resources to find other Zulu stories. Retell one in a small group.

FICTION | READER'S THEATRE

I Hope I Can

THINK ABOUT IT

Friendships can be challenging. What advice would you give someone who has had a disagreement with a friend?

WHEN GOING FOR your goals, it's important to have the support of others. Read what happens when Tallah doesn't get her friend's support.

CHARACTERS:
- Narrator
- Tallah
- Lexi
- Ms. Ashley

Narrator: More than anything, Tallah dreams of playing the lead in Applewood Public School's annual musical. Unfortunately, her friend Lexi doesn't think she has what it takes.

Tallah (*looking worried*): I know I can ... I know I can ... I know I can ...

Lexi (*walks up to Tallah in the hallway*): Why are you talking to yourself?

Tallah: I'm nervous! My audition for the school play is in 15 minutes. I'm really hoping to get the role of Guinevere.

Lexi: Oh. Really?

Tallah: What's *that* look for? You know I have always wanted to be in a play.

Lexi: *You've* always wanted to be in a play? Don't you remember what happened at summer camp?

Narrator: Tallah knows exactly what Lexi is talking about, though she's tried to forget it.

Lexi: It was your turn to recite the camp motto, so you walked to the front of the crowd. We waited for you to say something, but you were too scared.

Tallah (*looking down to the floor*): I remember.

Lexi: Then you started crying! The other kids kept calling you "crybaby" until I got the camp counsellors to put an end to it.

28

Tallah: Lexi, I was *eight* when that happened. I had never spoken in front of a crowd before. I was terrified!

Lexi: I'm just saying, you wouldn't want *that* to happen again!

Tallah: It won't happen again. I've been practising my lines all week.

Lexi: I'm not saying you shouldn't try out. I just think you should try out for a smaller role.

Narrator: Lexi and Tallah are friends, and they usually support each other. Tallah doesn't understand why Lexi isn't being supportive.

Tallah: But I want to play Guinevere. A little encouragement would be nice. I encouraged you when you tried out for the basketball team.

Lexi: That was different. Anyway, I'm outta here.

Narrator: Tallah and Lexi go their separate ways. Fifteen minutes later …

Ms. Ashley: That was wonderful, Tallah! We'll let you know when we've made a decision. Next up, Lexi Meyers!

Tallah: Lexi! You could have told me you were auditioning for Guinevere, too. That wasn't very nice.

> What character traits can be helpful when solving conflicts?

Lexi (*looks embarrassed*): Sorry, Tallah. I know it wasn't nice. I just thought that if you didn't try out, my chances would be better.

Tallah: I *knew* something wasn't right! Some friend you are!

Lexi: I know. I'm really sorry, Tallah. But I wanted to get the part so bad. I'm really sorry. I won't even try out.

Tallah: Nah, that's okay. Go ahead. And good luck. May the best Guinevere win!

CONNECT IT

Imagine you are a peer mediator at your school. What could you learn from Tallah when she wishes Lexi luck that you could use when helping others solve conflicts?

INFORMATIONAL TEXT | REPORT

No. 2 Construction Battalion

DREAMING OF

THINK ABOUT IT

Think about a time when you hoped to be part of something, but were not allowed. How did this situation make you feel?

WHEN WORLD WAR I (WWI) began in 1914, thousands of Canadian men rushed to enlist in the Canadian Expeditionary Force. By the time the war ended in 1918, 619 000 soldiers had enlisted. According to the Canadian War Museum, around seven percent of Canada's population was in uniform during WWI. Hundreds of thousands more supported the war effort from home.

African Canadians hoped to join the war effort, too. However, African Canadians were not allowed to be part of the armed forces. A group of determined Black men worked hard to change this. It took almost two years of protests and petitions, but, in 1916, the No. 2 Construction Battalion was formed. Read about it in this report.

EQUALITY

On 6 November 1914, Arthur Alexander, an African Canadian schoolteacher from North Buxton, Ontario, wrote a letter. His letter to Sam Hughes, the Minister of Militia and Defence said: "The coloured people of Canada want to know why they are not allowed to enlist in the Canadian militia. I am informed that several who have applied for enlistment in the Canadian Expeditionary Force have been refused for no other apparent reason than their colour, as they were physically and mentally fit." Alexander was just one of many Canadians who wanted to know why.

Arthur Alexander's letter to the Minister of Militia and Defence

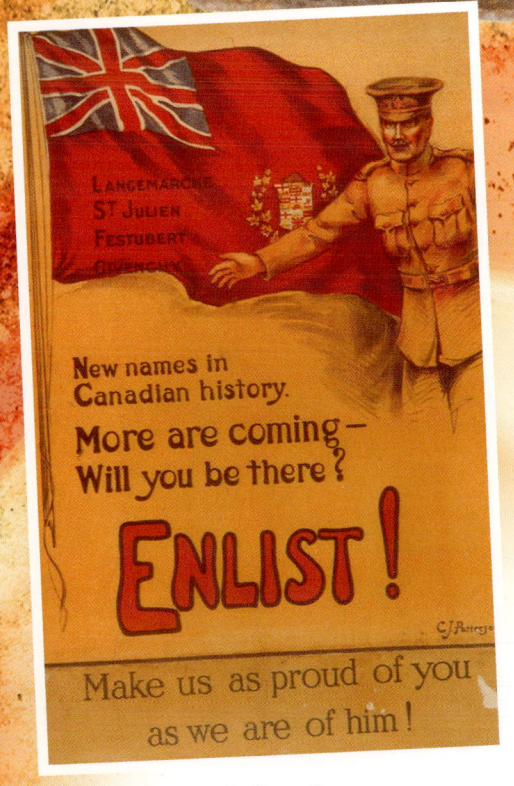

A Canadian recruiting poster

When WWI began in 1914, Canadians were excited about fighting alongside the British. Patriotism was high. Many men wanted to enlist as soldiers. According to Dr. Calvin Ruck, a former African Canadian senator, "Blacks were no exception. They were also seeking the adventure, the status, the glory, and the financial benefits" associated with going to war.

"Blacks were no exception. They were also seeking the adventure, the status, the glory, and the financial benefits" associated with going to war.

Sydney M. Jones was an African Canadian veteran of WWI. He recalled that enlisting was "the thing to do." However, because of the racism that existed in Canada, African Canadians were not allowed to enlist. In April 1916, Major-General Willoughby Gwatkin wrote of African Canadian soldiers, "In the trenches, he is not likely to make a good fighter; and the average White man will not associate with him on terms of equality." Because of these racist beliefs, African Canadians who wanted to serve were turned away. However, they kept pushing to be treated equally and to be allowed to serve their country. Because of this, an all-Black battalion was formed.

The No. 2 Construction Battalion was formed in Pictou, Nova Scotia, on 5 July 1916. More than 600 men joined it in 1916. Most were from Nova Scotia. They trained in Pictou and Truro, Nova Scotia. The officers in charge of the No. 2 Construction Battalion were all White, with the exception of the Battalion's chaplain, Reverend William Andrew White. White was one of the

Reverend William Andrew White, pictured in 1936, was the father of famous Canadian singer Portia White.

Patriotism: *love of one's country*
chaplain: *religious leader who provides spiritual help*

first commissioned officers of African Canadian heritage. During WWI, he was the only Black chaplain. His job was to give religious comfort to the men of No. 2 Construction Battalion.

Even after the No. 2 Construction Battalion was formed, African Canadian soldiers still faced prejudice. In 1917, the Battalion was sent to France, but the soldiers were not allowed to have combat roles. Instead, they were assigned to build roads, bridges, and shelters. They also served in the Canadian Forestry Corps, which provided lumber for building trenches and other structures.

African Canadians also contributed to the war effort on the home front. According to Veterans Affairs Canada, Black Canadians "helped achieve victory by working in factories making the weapons and supplies needed by the soldiers fighting overseas, and by taking part in patriotic activities like raising funds for the war effort."

WWI ended in 1918, and, two years later, the No. 2 Construction Battalion disbanded. While it lasted, the soldiers hoped and struggled for equality. Because they worked in unprotected areas of the war zone, some men were wounded and some lost their lives.

Though they're often not found in history books, the men of the No. 2 Construction Battalion made a significant contribution to Canada's role in WWI. They made it easier for men and women of African descent who dreamed of joining the armed forces to do so. By WWII, African Canadians were able to fight alongside other Canadian soldiers.

> Why do you think African Canadian soldiers were not allowed to have combat roles?

No. 2 Construction Battalion badges

commissioned: *having a high rank in the military*
disbanded: *broke up*

CONNECT IT

Use the Web and other resources to learn about the role of African Canadians in WWII or another war. Write a paragraph with your findings that could be added to this report. Remember to include the challenges and triumphs that these Canadians experienced in the war you chose to research.

FICTION | SHORT STORY

Becky and the WHEELS-AND-BRAKE BOYS

THINK ABOUT IT
Has there ever been something you really wanted, but weren't allowed to have? Tell a classmate about this experience.

BY JAMES BERRY

READ THIS SHORT STORY by James Berry to learn how far one young girl goes to achieve her biggest dream. Some of the story is written in patois, a way of speaking that is associated with a particular region.

ABOUT THE AUTHOR
James Berry was born in Jamaica in 1924. In 1948, he settled in England. He is a poet and author of short stories. In 1990, Berry became an Officer of the Order of the British Empire for his contributions to poetry.

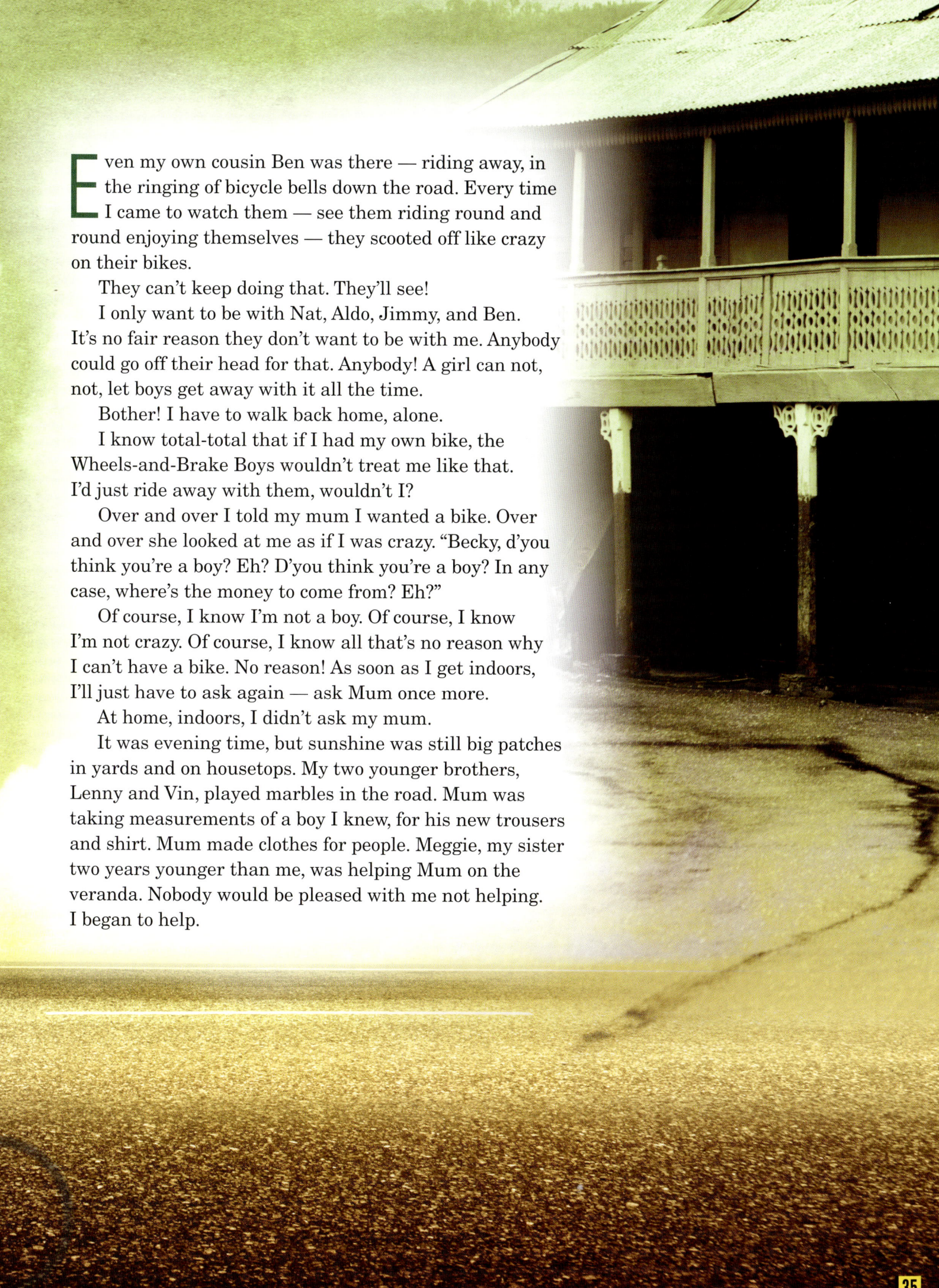

Even my own cousin Ben was there — riding away, in the ringing of bicycle bells down the road. Every time I came to watch them — see them riding round and round enjoying themselves — they scooted off like crazy on their bikes.

They can't keep doing that. They'll see!

I only want to be with Nat, Aldo, Jimmy, and Ben. It's no fair reason they don't want to be with me. Anybody could go off their head for that. Anybody! A girl can not, not, let boys get away with it all the time.

Bother! I have to walk back home, alone.

I know total-total that if I had my own bike, the Wheels-and-Brake Boys wouldn't treat me like that. I'd just ride away with them, wouldn't I?

Over and over I told my mum I wanted a bike. Over and over she looked at me as if I was crazy. "Becky, d'you think you're a boy? Eh? D'you think you're a boy? In any case, where's the money to come from? Eh?"

Of course, I know I'm not a boy. Of course, I know I'm not crazy. Of course, I know all that's no reason why I can't have a bike. No reason! As soon as I get indoors, I'll just have to ask again — ask Mum once more.

At home, indoors, I didn't ask my mum.

It was evening time, but sunshine was still big patches in yards and on housetops. My two younger brothers, Lenny and Vin, played marbles in the road. Mum was taking measurements of a boy I knew, for his new trousers and shirt. Mum made clothes for people. Meggie, my sister two years younger than me, was helping Mum on the veranda. Nobody would be pleased with me not helping. I began to help.

Granny-Liz would always stop fanning herself to drink up a glass of ice water. I gave my granny a glass of ice water, there in her rocking chair. I looked in the kitchen to find shelled coconut pieces to cut into small cubes for the fowls' morning feed. But Granny-Liz had done it. I came and started tidying up bits and pieces of cut-off material around my mum on the floor. My sister got nasty, saying she was already helping Mum. Not a single good thing was happening for me.

With me being all so thoughtful of Granny's need of a cool drink, she started up some botheration against me.

Listen to Granny-Liz: "Becky, with you moving about me here on the veranda, I hope you dohn have any centipedes or scorpions in a jam jar in your pocket."

> "Botheration" means trouble. What other words could Granny-Liz have used here?

"Those boys are a menace. ... they're heading for trouble."

"No, mam," I said sighing, trying to be calm. "Granny-Liz," I went on, "you forgot. My centipede and scorpion died." All the same, storm broke against me.

"Becky," my mum said. "You know I don't like you wandering off after dinner. Haven't I told you I don't want you keeping company with those awful riding-about bicycle boys? Eh?"

"Yes, mam."

"Those boys are a menace. Riding bicycles on sidewalks and narrow paths together, ringing bicycle bells and braking at people's feet like wild bulls charging anybody, they're heading for trouble."

"They're the Wheels-and-Brake Boys, mam."

"The what?"

"The Wheels-and-Brake Boys."

"Oh! Given themselves a name as well, have they? Well, Becky, answer this. How d'you always manage to look like you just escaped from a hair-pulling battle? Eh? And don't I tell you not to break the backs down and wear your canvas shoes like slippers? Don't you ever hear what I say?"

"Yes, mam."

"D'you want to end up a field labourer? Like where your father used to be overseer?"

"No, mam."

"Well, Becky, will you please go off and do your homework?"

Everybody did everything to stop me. I was allowed no chance whatsoever. No chance to talk to Mum about the bike I dream of day and night. And I knew exactly the bike I wanted. I wanted a bike like Ben's bike. Oh, I wished I still had even my scorpion on a string to run up and down somebody's back!

I answered my mum. "Yes, mam." I went off into Meg's and my bedroom.

I sat down at the little table, as well as I might. Could homework stay in anybody's head in broad daylight outside? No. Could I keep a bike like Ben's out of my head? Not one bit. That bike took me all over the place. My beautiful bike jumped every log, every rock, every fence. My beautiful bike did everything cleverer than a clever cowboy's horse, with me in the saddle. And the bell, the bell was such a glorious gong of a ring!

If Dad was alive, I could talk to him. If Dad was alive, he'd give me money for the bike like a shot.

I sighed. It was amazing what a sigh could do. I sighed and tumbled on a great idea. Tomorrow evening, I'd get Shirnette to come with me. Both of us together would be sure to get the boys interested to teach us to ride. Wow! With Shirnette, they can't just ride away!

Next day at school, everything went sour. For the first time, Shirnette and me had a real fight, because of what I hated most.

Shirnette brought a cockroach to school in a shoe-polish tin. At playtime, she opened the tin and let the cockroach fly into my blouse. Pure panic and disgust nearly killed me. I crushed up the cockroach in my clothes and practically ripped my blouse off, there in open sunlight. Oh, the smell of a cockroach is the nastiest ever to block your nose! I started running with my blouse to go and wash it. Twice, I had to stop and be sick.

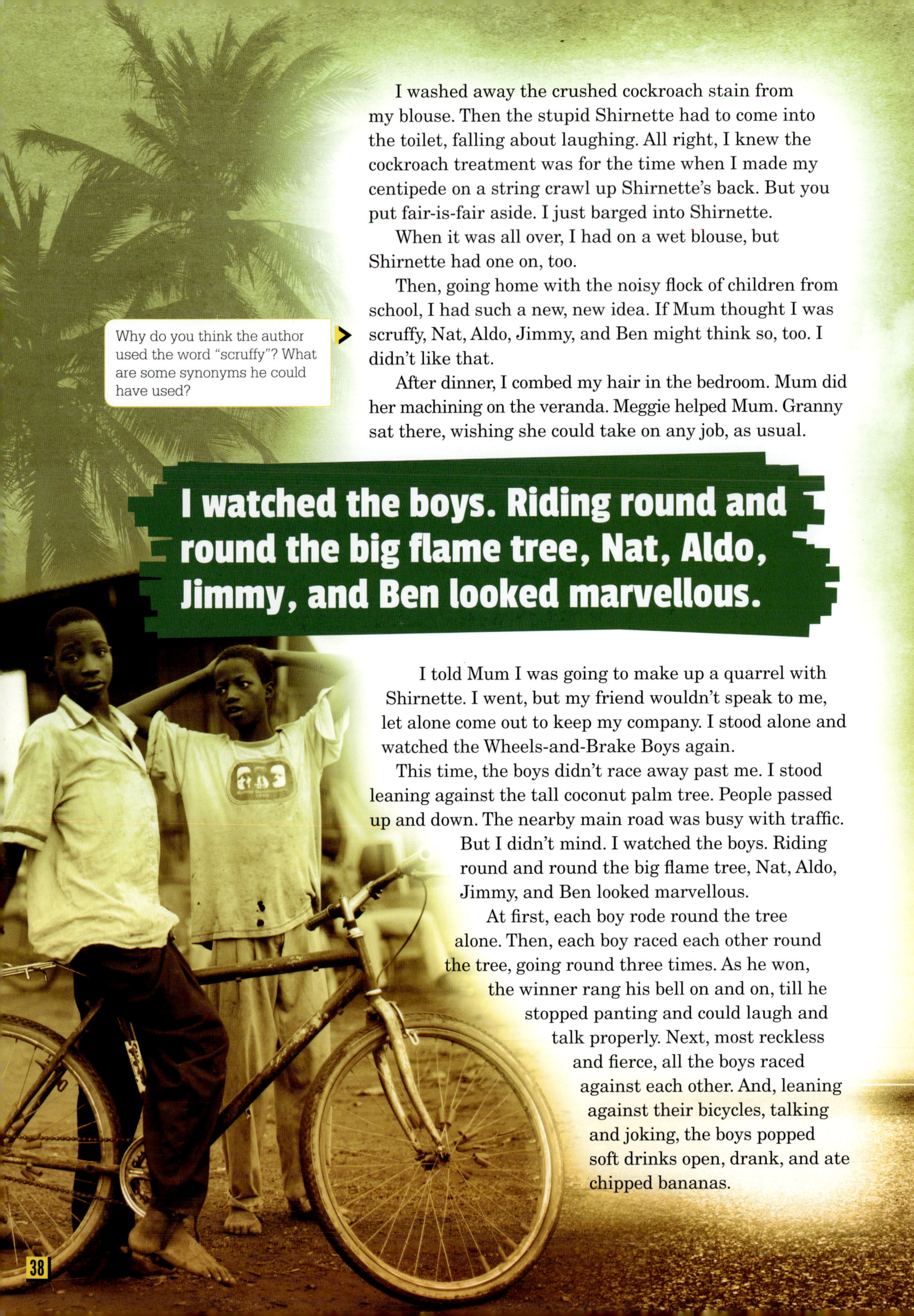

I washed away the crushed cockroach stain from my blouse. Then the stupid Shirnette had to come into the toilet, falling about laughing. All right, I knew the cockroach treatment was for the time when I made my centipede on a string crawl up Shirnette's back. But you put fair-is-fair aside. I just barged into Shirnette.

When it was all over, I had on a wet blouse, but Shirnette had one on, too.

Then, going home with the noisy flock of children from school, I had such a new, new idea. If Mum thought I was scruffy, Nat, Aldo, Jimmy, and Ben might think so, too. I didn't like that.

After dinner, I combed my hair in the bedroom. Mum did her machining on the veranda. Meggie helped Mum. Granny sat there, wishing she could take on any job, as usual.

> Why do you think the author used the word "scruffy"? What are some synonyms he could have used?

I watched the boys. Riding round and round the big flame tree, Nat, Aldo, Jimmy, and Ben looked marvellous.

I told Mum I was going to make up a quarrel with Shirnette. I went, but my friend wouldn't speak to me, let alone come out to keep my company. I stood alone and watched the Wheels-and-Brake Boys again.

This time, the boys didn't race away past me. I stood leaning against the tall coconut palm tree. People passed up and down. The nearby main road was busy with traffic.

But I didn't mind. I watched the boys. Riding round and round the big flame tree, Nat, Aldo, Jimmy, and Ben looked marvellous.

At first, each boy rode round the tree alone. Then, each boy raced each other round the tree, going round three times. As he won, the winner rang his bell on and on, till he stopped panting and could laugh and talk properly. Next, most reckless and fierce, all the boys raced against each other. And, leaning against their bicycles, talking and joking, the boys popped soft drinks open, drank, and ate chipped bananas.

I walked up to Nat, Aldo, Jimmy, and Ben and said, "Can somebody teach me to ride?"

"Why don't you stay indoors and learn to cook and sew and wash clothes?" Jimmy said.

I grinned. "I know that all already," I said. "And one day, perhaps I'll even be mum to a boy child, like all of you. Can you cook and sew and wash clothes, Jimmy? All I want is to learn to ride. I want you to teach me."

I didn't know why I said what I said. But everybody went silent and serious.

One after the other, Nat, Aldo, Jimmy, and Ben got on their bikes and rode off. I wasn't at all cross with them. I only wanted to be riding out of the playground with them. I knew they'd be heading into the town to have ice cream and things and talk and laugh.

Mum was sitting alone on the veranda. She sewed buttons onto a white shirt she'd made. I sat down next to Mum. Straightaway, "Mum," I said, "I still want to have a bike badly."

"Oh, Becky, you still have that foolishness in your head? What am I going to do?"

Mum talked with some sympathy. Mum knew I was honest. "I can't get rid of it, mam," I said.

Mum stopped sewing. "Becky," she said, staring in my face, "how many girls around here do you see with bicycles?"

I knew Mum was just about to give in.

"Janice Gordon has a bike," I reminded her.

"Janice Gordon's dad has acres and acres of coconuts and bananas, with a business in the town as well."

I knew Mum was just about to give in. Then my granny had to come out onto the veranda and interfere. Listen to that Granny-Liz. "Becky, I heard you mother tell you over and over she cahn afford to buy you a bike. Yet you keep on and on. Child, you're a girl."

"But I don't want a bike because I'm a girl."

"D'you want it because you feel like a bwoy?" Granny said.

Granny just carried on. "A tomboy's like a whistling woman and a crowing hen, who can only come to a bad end. D'you understand?"

> What is your opinion of the attitude that Becky can't have a bike because she's a girl?

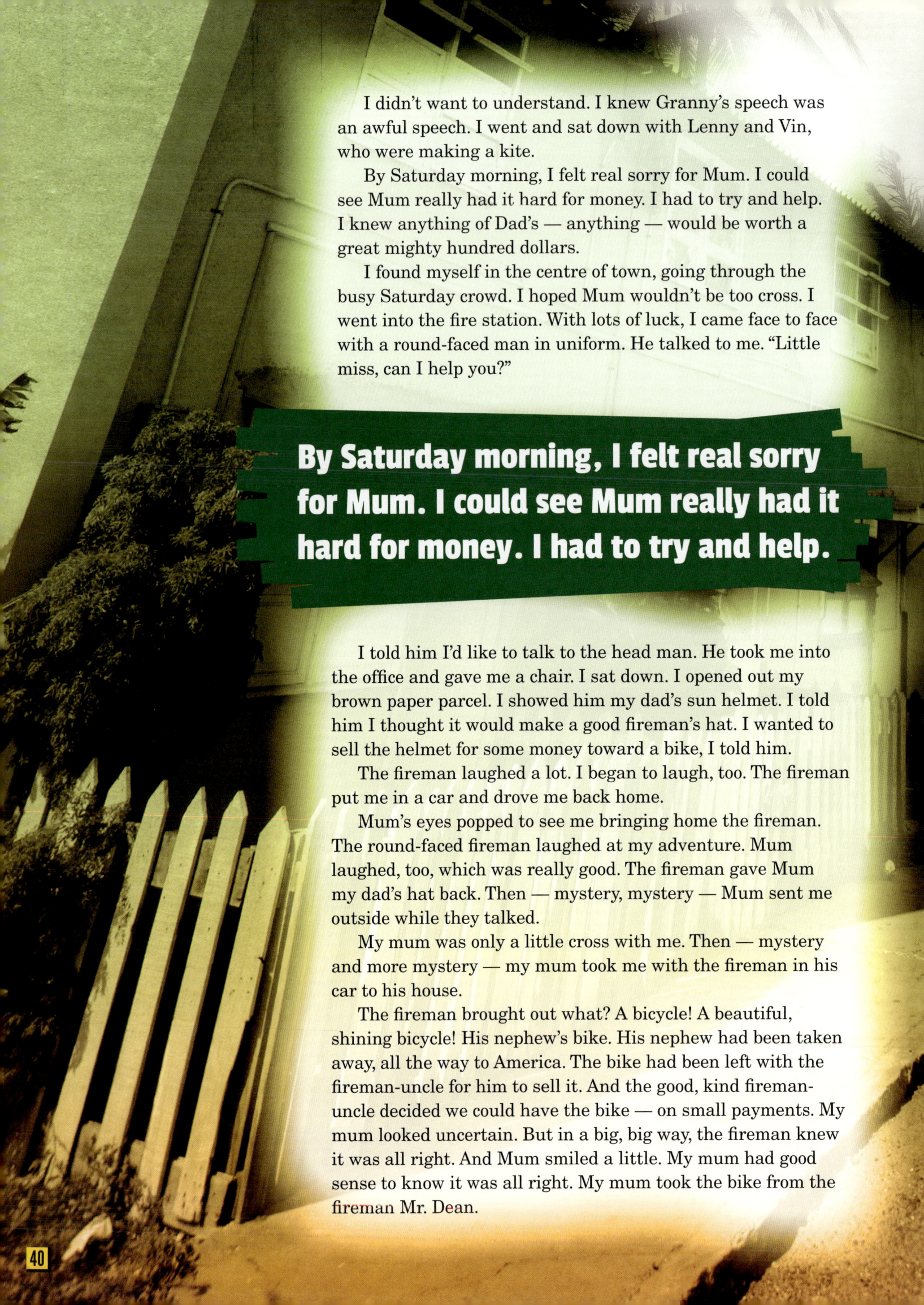

I didn't want to understand. I knew Granny's speech was an awful speech. I went and sat down with Lenny and Vin, who were making a kite.

By Saturday morning, I felt real sorry for Mum. I could see Mum really had it hard for money. I had to try and help. I knew anything of Dad's — anything — would be worth a great mighty hundred dollars.

I found myself in the centre of town, going through the busy Saturday crowd. I hoped Mum wouldn't be too cross. I went into the fire station. With lots of luck, I came face to face with a round-faced man in uniform. He talked to me. "Little miss, can I help you?"

> **By Saturday morning, I felt real sorry for Mum. I could see Mum really had it hard for money. I had to try and help.**

I told him I'd like to talk to the head man. He took me into the office and gave me a chair. I sat down. I opened out my brown paper parcel. I showed him my dad's sun helmet. I told him I thought it would make a good fireman's hat. I wanted to sell the helmet for some money toward a bike, I told him.

The fireman laughed a lot. I began to laugh, too. The fireman put me in a car and drove me back home.

Mum's eyes popped to see me bringing home the fireman. The round-faced fireman laughed at my adventure. Mum laughed, too, which was really good. The fireman gave Mum my dad's hat back. Then — mystery, mystery — Mum sent me outside while they talked.

My mum was only a little cross with me. Then — mystery and more mystery — my mum took me with the fireman in his car to his house.

The fireman brought out what? A bicycle! A beautiful, shining bicycle! His nephew's bike. His nephew had been taken away, all the way to America. The bike had been left with the fireman-uncle for him to sell it. And the good, kind fireman-uncle decided we could have the bike — on small payments. My mum looked uncertain. But in a big, big way, the fireman knew it was all right. And Mum smiled a little. My mum had good sense to know it was all right. My mum took the bike from the fireman Mr. Dean.

And guess what? Seeing my bike much, much newer than his, my cousin Ben's eyes popped with envy. But he took on the big job. He taught me to ride. Then he taught Shirnette.

I ride into town with the Wheels-and-Brake Boys now. When she can borrow a bike, Shirnette comes, too. We all sit together. We have patties and ice cream and drink drinks together. We talk and joke. We ride about, all over the place.

And, again, guess what? Fireman Mr. Dean became our best friend, and Mum's especially. He started coming around almost every day.

CONNECT IT

What do you think happens after this story finishes? Write a paragraph about what happens next to continue the story.

INFORMATIONAL TEXT | PROFILE

RACING TO THE FINISH

THINK ABOUT IT

What do you know about the Paralympics? What do you think is the significance of the Paralympics for the athletes, for sports, and for our society? Talk about the Paralympics in a small group.

BRAEDON DOLFO WON'T let the fact that he is partially blind stop him from achieving his dreams. Learn all about him in this profile.

Braedon Dolfo is best known for his enormous success in the world of track and field. But his inspirational story doesn't start or stop there.

Dolfo was born in Kingstown, on the Caribbean island of St. Vincent. When he was 18 months old, he was adopted by Coquitlam, British Columbia, residents Brent and Diana Dolfo. The family moved to nearby Langley.

When Dolfo was only five years old, he developed cataracts, a condition that clouds the lens behind the iris of the eye. This condition is more commonly seen in people who are much older. During this time, Dolfo also developed another eye condition called chronic uveitis. He was later diagnosed with glaucoma, a disease that eventually caused Dolfo to lose most of his vision when he was only 11 years old.

"The sacrifice is definitely worth the reward. ... What 18-year-old gets to go to the Olympics?"

Despite the obstacles he faced, Dolfo did not give up on his dream of becoming a track and field athlete. In 2010, he joined the Canadian para-athletic national team. In 2011, he won the bronze medal for high jump at the 2011 International Paralympic Committee (IPC) World Championships in New Zealand. He also won another bronze medal at the Parapan American Games in a 100-metre race.

At just 18 years old, Dolfo's skill and determination paid off when he represented Canada at London's 2012 Paralympic Games. When asked how this felt, Dolfo said, "The sacrifice is definitely worth the reward. ... What 18-year-old gets to go to the Olympics?"

Braedon Dolfo competes at the 2012 London Paralympics.

Dolfo's positive attitude and drive helped him finish seventh in the race with a time of 11.27 seconds, just a millisecond away from his personal best and Canadian record of 11.26 seconds. After finishing the race, Dolfo told reporters, "To finish seventh in the world is a blessing."

After his amazing performance at the Paralympic Games, Dolfo achieved a new Canadian record of 11.22 seconds during a semifinal race at the IPC World Championships in July 2013. He also won a bronze medal at the 2013 Pan American Junior Championships. In the same year, he won gold medals in both the 200-metre and 400-metre races at home in the British Columbia High School provincial championships. In December 2013, Dolfo won the BC Athletics Award for Para-athletics Male Athlete of the Year.

In 2012, Dolfo began attending Trinity Western University. While at school, he balances studying and being a member of the track and field team.

Even after all of his amazing accomplishments, Dolfo is still focused on striving for more. He is currently training for the IPC World Championships in 2015 in Doha, Qatar, and the summer Parapan American Games in Toronto. In 2016, he hopes to win a medal at the Paralympic Games in Rio de Janeiro, Brazil.

Dolfo hopes to be an inspiration to other athletes with big dreams.

"You get to see little kids smiling and coming up to you and asking for pictures and autographs," he says. Even with all of his achievements, Dolfo has not let his success or fame go to his head. "It means the world to them, and it really means the world to you. You are inspiring people."

Dolfo runs at the 2011 Parapan American Games in Guadalajara, Mexico.

Braedon Dolfo uses Twitter to inspire others. Here are just a few of his inspiring tweets.

Braedon Dolfo @BDolfo93
Keep it real and step into new challenges every day

Braedon Dolfo @BDolfo93
Vast ocean views are motion pictures of dreams that can't go wrong

Braedon Dolfo @BDolfo93
Be elevated — It's not about competing against anyone else, it's just about competing against yourself to better your personal best

Braedon Dolfo @BDolfo93
The realization that searching for greater happiness sometimes appears in front of you every day, whether it's family, friends, pets, or more

CONNECT IT

Imagine you are a writer for a sports magazine who is going to interview Braedon Dolfo. Write a list of five questions you would like to ask him. Make sure you include a question about his hopes and dreams. With a partner, role-play the interview.

INFORMATIONAL TEXT | PERSONAL ACCOUNT

WINNERS Never Quit

BY LISA NICHOLS

THINK ABOUT IT

Think about a time when you decided to quit doing something like a hobby or playing a sport. Were you happy with your decision? Talk with a classmate about why you made that decision.

IT OFTEN TAKES hard work to achieve our dreams. Athletes train for years for a chance to compete in international games. But some athletes just love to play the game. Read about one athlete who wrestled with the decision to quit swimming because she thought she wasn't good enough.

I had been swimming competitively for about five years and was ready to quit, not because I had satisfied my desire to swim, but because I felt I was horrible at it. I was often the only African American at a swim competition, and our team could not afford anything close to the great uniforms the other teams were wearing. Worst of all, though, and my number-one reason for wanting to quit, was that I kept receiving "honourable mentions" at each competition, which simply means, "Thank you for coming. You did not even rank first, second, or third, but we don't want you to go home with nothing, so here is something to hide later." Any athlete knows that you don't want to have a bookshelf or a photo album full of "honourable mentions." They call that the "show-up ribbon"; you get one just because you showed up.

One hot summer day, the very day before a big swim meet, I decided to break the news to my grandma that I was quitting the swim team. On the one hand, I thought it was a big deal because I was the only athlete in the family, but on the other hand, because no one ever came to see me compete, I didn't think it would be a major issue. You have to know my grandma — she stood on tiptoe to five feet two inches and weighed a maximum 95 pounds [43 kg], but could run the entire operation of her house without ever leaving her sofa or raising her voice. As I sat next to my grandma, I assumed my usual position of laying my big head on her tiny little lap so that she could rub it.

When I told her of my desire to quit swimming, she abruptly pushed my head off of her lap, sat me straight up facing her, and said, "Baby, remember these words: 'A quitter never wins and a winner never quits.' Your grandmother didn't raise no losers or quitters. You go to that swim meet tomorrow, and you swim like you are a grandchild of mine, you hear?"

I was too afraid to say anything but "Yes, ma'am."

The next day, we arrived at the swim meet late, missing my group of swimmers in the 15/16 age group. My coach insisted I be allowed to swim with the next group, the next age older. I could have just as easily crawled out of the gym. I knew she was including me in the race so our long drive would not be wasted, and she had no expectations whatsoever that I would come in anything but eighth — and only that because there were not nine lanes.

As I mounted the board, I quickly noticed that these girls with their skintight caps, goggles, and Speedo suits were here to do one thing — kick my chocolate butt!

All of a sudden, my grandma's words rang in my head, *Quitters never win and winners never quit, quitters never win and winners never quit.*

SPLASH!

Quitters never win and winners never quit, quitters never win and winners never quit.

I was swimming harder than I'd ever swum before. As I drew my right arm back, I noticed I was tied with one person. I assumed we were battling for eighth place and I refused to finish dead last, so I added more kick on the last 200 yards [183 m].

Quitters never win and winners never quit, quitters never win and winners never quit.

I hit the wall and looked to the left and to the right for the swimmers who had beat me, but no one was there. They must have gotten out of the water already.

I raised my head to see my coach screaming hysterically. My eyes followed her pointing finger, and I couldn't believe what I saw. The other swimmers had just reached the halfway point of the pool! That day, at age 15, I broke the national 17/18-year-old 50-freestyle record. I hung up my honourable mentions and replaced them with a huge trophy.

Back at Grandma's, I laid my head on her lap and told her about our great race.

Lisa Nichols is now an award-winning motivational speaker, author, and coach.

CONNECT IT

Make a poster that features the quotation "Quitters never win and winners never quit." If you would prefer, you can choose your own inspirational quotation. Include pictures and illustrations on your poster. Tell a classmate why you chose each one.

Index

A
accomplishment, 7–10, 12, 19, 44
achievement, 4–5, 9, 11–12, 15, 18, 23, 33–34, 42, 44, 46
advice, 4, 10–11, 28
Alexander, Arthur, 31
athlete, 42–44, 46
attitude, 39, 44
Augustine, Jean, 8–10

B
Berry, James, 34
Butterfield, Joan, 12–13

C
Canadian Expeditionary Force, 30–31
career, 8, 11
celebration, 18–21
challenges, 13, 17–18, 21, 33, 45
community, 8–9, 16, 19, 23
contribution, 23, 33–34
courage, 6, 13, 21

D
determination, 13, 30, 43
difficulty, 14–15, 22, 26
Dolfo, Braedon, 42–45
Drummond, Dwight, 14–17

E
education, 8, 10–11, 15, 18–19
effort, 18–19, 30, 33
employment, 15, 21, 23
encouragement, 8, 23, 29

F
faith, 13

G
goals, 11, 28
Godefa, Hannah, 18–19

H
hardship, 9, 16

I
innovation, 10, 18
inspiration, 6, 8, 10, 42, 44–45, 47
interest, 11, 37
International Women's Day, 20–21

J
Jean, Michaëlle, 20–23
job, 9, 11, 14, 17, 21, 23, 33, 38, 41

L
leadership, 11, 18–19, 32
limit, 7, 22

M
Member of Parliament, 9, 19
MOSAIC, 20–21, 23

N
newsroom, 17
No. 2 Construction Battalion, 30–33

O
obstacle, 4, 9, 12, 22, 43
opportunity, 15, 19, 22–23
organization, 9, 18–20

P
Paralympics, 42–43
passion, 7, 9, 16, 19, 23
possibilities, 23
potential, 19, 23
poverty, 9, 18–19

Q
quitting, 46–47

R
responsibilities, 23

S
sacrifice, 7, 14, 43
Sirleaf, Ellen Johnson, 4
skill, 11, 43
spirit, 18–19, 21, 32
success, 6, 8, 17, 42, 44
support, 9, 19, 28–30

T
teamwork, 11

V
volunteering, 9, 23

Acknowledgements

The publisher gratefully acknowledges the following for permission to reprint copyrighted material in this book.

- Augustine, The Honourable Jean. Honorary Doctorate acceptance speech at York University, 17 July 2011. Reprinted with permission.

"Becky and the Wheels-and-Brake Boys," from *A Thief in the Village, and Other Stories of Jamaica* by James Berry. Reprinted with permission of Peters, Fraser & Dunlop (www.petersfraserdunlop.com) on behalf of James Berry.

Butterfield, Joan. "Beyond the Rhythm," from *COLOURblind: Association of African-Canadian Artists*, 2009. Permission courtesy of the author.

Elayadathusseril, Gloria. "Dwight Drummond, Anchor man," from *Canadian Immigrant*, 19 May 2011. Reprinted with permission from *Canadian Immigrant* magazine (www.canadianimmigrant.ca).

Extract from letter: Arthur Alexander to Sir Sam Hughes regarding coloured enlistment in army. Source: Library and Archives Canada/Department of Militia and Defence fonds/RG24, Vol 1206, File HQ297-1-21, Alexander to Hughes, 6 November 1914.

Getachew, Samuel. "The One Canadian I Admire And Will Celebrate Today," from *Huffington Post*, 23 January 2014. Permission courtesy of the author.

"Her Excellency the Right Honourable Michaëlle Jean on the Occasion of the 30th Anniversary of MOSAIC." Courtesy of Rideau Hall © Her Majesty The Queen in Right of Canada represented by the Office of the Secretary to the Governor General (2006). Reproduced with the permission of the Office of the Secretary to the Governor General (2014).

Nichols, Lisa. "Winners Never Quit," from *Chicken Soup for the African-American Soul*. © Lisa Nichols. Permission courtesy of the author.

Photo Sources
Cover: splats–Keo/Shutterstock.com; **4:** glitter–tomer turjeman/Shutterstock.com; ribbons–iStockphoto.com/© DNY59; **6:** stars background–pixelparticle/Shutterstock.com; Measha Brueggergosman–Keith Beaty / GetStock.com; Barack Obama–Official White House Photo by Pete Souza **7:** Portia White–Toronto Star Archives / GetStock.com; Donovan Bailey–© PA Wire/PA Photos/KEYSTONE Press; Lupita Nyong'o–Jaguar PS/Shutterstock.com; **8:** [blur–Soleiko; yellow lines–Nik Merkulov; wood texture–Reinhold Leitner] Shutterstock.com; **9:** Jean Augustine–Charla Jones / GetStock.com **11:** [markerboard–nrt; note papers–Picsfive] Shutterstock.com; **12:** abstract paint–Dariusz Gudowicz/Shutterstock.com; Joan Butterfield–courtesy of Joan Butterfield; **13:** Izzy Ohiro paintings–Artwork by Izzy Ohiro/Provided by Joan Butterfield AACA; **14:** lines–pixelparticle/Shutterstock.com; Dwight Drummond–Andrew Wallace / GetStock.com; **15:** camera–withGod/Shutterstock.com; **16:** Mediwake and Drummond–Andrew Wallace / GetStock.com; **17:** camera operator–iStockphoto.com/© GeorgeManga; stage lights–Jackfoto/Shutterstock.com; **18:** [texture–RoyStudio.eu; schoolgirls–Arapov Sergey] Shutterstock.com; **19:** pencil–Melinda Fawver/Shutterstock.com; Hannah Godefa–STAN HONDA/AFP/Getty Images; school–Ji-Elle; **20:** paper texture–The_Pixel/Shutterstock.com; Michaëlle Jean–ChinaFotoPress/Getty Images; **21:** Mlle Marie-Eden and Michaëlle Jean–ROTA/Anwar Hussein Collection/Getty Images; **22:** students–Toronto Star / GetStock.com; **24:** illustrations–Megan Little; **28:** [dotted gradient–Beluza Ludmilal; school–Brian Guest; girl–bikeriderlondon; purple girl–tmcphotos] Shutterstock.com; **30:** background–Antti Sompinmäki/Shutterstock.com; No. 2 Construction Battalion–Windsor's Community Museum P6110; **31:** wood–My Life Graphic/Shutterstock.com; letter–Library Archives of Canada; **32:** Enlist poster–Library Archives of Canada; Rev. William A. White–National Archives of Canada; photo album–Lukiyanova Natalia / frenta/Shutterstock.com; **33:** badge–CP PHOTO/Andrew Vaughan/CP Images; **34:** [palm trees–PRILL; girl–Daniel Korzeniewski; sky–Elenamiv; road–Iakov Kalinin; cyclists–grynold] Shutterstock.com; James Berry–Photograph by Fay Godwin/© The British Library Board; **35:** [house–iStockphoto.com/© peeterv; **36:** bridge iStockphoto.com/© peeterv; wheel–Gena73/Shutterstock.com; **37:** girl–Daniel Korzeniewski/Shutterstock.com; **38:** boys and bike–iStockphoto.com/© UygarGeographic Photography; **39:** bike riding–Exactostock / SuperStock; **40:** houses–iStockphoto.com/© ruffraido; **41:** [girl–Daniel Korzeniewski; bike–chevanon] Shutterstock.com; **42:** [track–leungchopan; pattern–ColorsArk] Shutterstock.com; **43:** Braedon Dolfo–Phillip MacCallum/© Canadian Paralympic Committee; **44:** Braedon Dolfo–Matthew Murnaghan/© Canadian Paralympic Committee; **46:** water–mythja/Shutterstock.com; **47:** Lisa Nichos–© 2010-2014 Motivating The Masses/motivatingthemasses.com; swimmers–jeep2499/Shutterstock.com.